Top of My Lungs

Top of My Lungs

Poems and Paintings

AND THE ESSAY
"How Poetry Saved My Life"

Natalie Goldberg

THE OVERLOOK PRESS
Woodstock & New York

First published in the United States in 2002 by
The Overlook Press, Peter Mayer Publishers, Inc.
Woodstock & New York

WOODSTOCK:
One Overlook Drive
Woodstock, NY 12498
www.overlookpress.com
[for individual orders, bulk and special sales, contact our Woodstock office]

NEW YORK:
141 Wooster Street
New York, NY 10012

Some of the poems in this book were first published in *American Jewish
World, Bright Water, Calyx, Crow Call Press, The Lake Street Review, Living Color,
Milkweed Chronicle, Minnesota Monthly, Puerto del Sol, Shambhala Sun, Banana Rose,
Another Desert: An Anthology, Chokecherries 1999,* and *Chokecherries 2000.*

Thank you to the Bush Foundation, which gave me a poetry fellowship
and a year's time to write many of these poems.

The paintings in this book have not been previously published in book form

Library of Congress Cataloging-in-Publication Data

Goldberg, Natallie.
Top of my lungs / Natalie Goldberg.
p. cm.
I. Title.
PS3557.O3583 T67 2002   813'.54—dc21   2002025809

Book design and type formatting by Bernard Schleifer
Printed in the United States of America
ISBN 1-58567-298-X
9 8 7 6 5 4 3 2 1

For my grandparents
        Rose and Sam Edelstein
        who I adored
and for my father's people
        Nathan and Rose
        who I never met

Contents

(Painting titles are in italics)

How Poetry Saved My Life

I WAS IN MY EARLY TWENTIES and knew nothing but a hunger, a wild restlessness, an unease. I had no landing place and no direction after I graduated from college with a BA in English and found no one who wanted to hire me for the sake of literature, the one thing I loved faithfully since ninth grade. No one even seemed to value it. I was bewildered and out on my own in the big, non-matriculated world.

Then one exquisite October afternoon, sitting on a futon in a communal house on the corner of Hill and Olivia in Ann Arbor, Michigan, in 1972, I experienced time collapse and space move into rivers. The walls exploded into a bath of black crows and electricity passed through my burning hand. No longer did I push words around on a page. A town, a bakery on a street, a friendship I once loved, all shimmered. A holy thing had happened. I had written my first true poem. Poetry was no longer relegated only to the realm of dead white men from the seventeenth century who had lived across the ocean and filled my classroom textbooks. Poetry was mine. A synapse had connected. I could write.

For the first time I noticed trees and flowers. I learned names: Russian olive, elm, oak, peony, geranium, petunia, marigold. Details mattered. Cracks on sidewalks, broken glass, worn stop signs, everything spoke to me. Rock, leaf, car. I rode rushes of thought with my cheap pen. I gripped a spiral notebook.

Poetry, I whispered, poetry.

My mind extended over clouds, insects, birds, small lost countries. I now had a purpose, a direction. My grandmother's soup exposed layers of possibility, my father's white starched shirt held my attention. Tomato soup, Brillo, World War II, ceiling paint, Ohio, this knee, that clock, his ring, all had weight and gravity. A kiss was no longer just a kiss— let it crack open a line for me. Let my heart break. I knew nothing. I received it all.

Before poetry, I was lost. Now loss had a smell, a color, a texture. A fast train could split its side. I held lost childhood, lost shoe, lost moment. They belonged to me and I was found.

There was nothing I couldn't speak about. My most mundane experience could take shape. If I peeled a grape, land slid in Caracas. If I bought a pair of pants, there was rain in the Sahara. Do you see it? A woman mattered. She had muscle and the force of storms.

Poetry was my way into the big religion. It split open language, grammar, broke down objects and subjects. I swayed as one with chimneys, sycamores, the hungry, and the hurt. History resounded. Memory lost the past and arrived in the present. My eyes were awake underwater. Was the poem writing me or was I breathing the poem? I was free to be buried, to be forgotten, or I could live forever in the rise and fall of the Pacific tide.

I went to cafés, readings, bookstores. I met friends who loved what I loved. We bent our heads over the Mississippi, counted eight sparrows on a fire escape. I was introduced to a half-known poet, soon to die. I watched him eat a thin ham sandwich at a drugstore. He slowly mouthed: "Poetry will never fail you, but you may fail poetry." I held Jim White's words down deep inside as his body was returned to his beloved Indianapolis.

And then I used his words to move me: I hitched to Chicago to hear one of the first poetry slam contests, studied with Allen Ginsberg in Boulder, Colorado, wanted to follow in his hallowed footsteps, met Anne Waldman, Ntozake Shange, heard Linda Gregg, Louise Gluck, Nikki Giovanni, Galway Kinnell, Gerald Stern, Amiri Baraka, Miguel Algarin, Simon Ortiz, Marge Piercy, read Adrienne Rich, Denise Levertov, May Swenson, Anne Sexton, James Wright, Gwendolyn Brooks, Maxine Kumin.

I won a poetry fellowship and traveled to Israel, heard ancient Hebrew spoken in the streets, walked with Bedouins and camels in Sinai, beheld an oasis of three pomegranate trees against hills of pink sand. I attended readings in Jerusalem where people came after work, their lunch pails still in their hands. I sat and watched as the question and answer period lasted longer than the reading. "Why did you put 'the' in the third line?" I saw that a country could honor its poets, that poetry was available to everyone, and that it was an esteemed profession.

When I met an Israeli, even in the street, and they heard I was a writer, they said, "Recite one of your poems right now" and I memorized my poems so I could do that. A new and different voice came to me in that land, straight from the root of my life and I was not ashamed. I read to a group of scientists in Tel Aviv my last night in that old, old country. I was no longer divided by any border or boundary.

I returned home and when I began to write prose, poetry was my foundation. It taught me the care and profundity of each word. It demanded that I not be glib, that my whole body stand behind what I said. Poetry glimmered between the branches of my sentences, the one thing in our greedy society that has not been gobbled up and sold in the marketplace. Always at my back, it kept me honest and served as an incorruptible reminder.

I dedicated myself to something bigger than myself and was handed over to beings seen and unseen, mountains and space, dead ghosts, grocery stores, night owls, snow, whistles, the divine in the center of the dumb. I came to love my life, its ragged edges, big hours, and lonesome paths. I learned that one equals two, three, then four blue apples, seven pears, until it comes back to itself again. All one intimate, aching poem. All of us. That's what poetry taught me and how it saved my life.

What a poet finally passes on is her breath at moments of inspiration. We read the work aloud and breathe her breath. May you feel inspired by these poems and may they help to bring you home.

Morning, Florida (1999)

When You Leave Home

You leave behind everything you will ever know
about the world
its dark color its daffodil lining
you won't see anything else
but their forms over and over
in the streets and trees
Branches reach out to you
with your peculiar last name in a funny country
and all you carry
you left behind
in the warm bed under the old quilt
below the leaky roof.

Coke and Chickens

Two million coke bottles did not die in the heat wave that struck Texas like an old chicken thrown against a barn. Kids in red pickups, winding down dusty roads in Texas this summer, looked for coke and avoided chicken. The old people, whose blood boiled when the heat hit 110, didn't want any poultry. Even the chickens didn't want coke when they croaked.

The price of chicken has gone up this summer like the heat in Texas from 69 cents a pound to 89 cents. Coke has always been overpriced. It didn't rise with the heat. Get a chicken near a hot lake in Texas during the heat wave and you've got soup. When a coke's empty you still have the bottle. When a chicken is dead, you have bones. Put the bones in the bottle and you have a sculpture. Put a chicken next to a bottle of coke in a heat wave and I bet you $10 the chicken will move first.

It wasn't so good for Texas this summer. A hurricane in the south and chickens collapsing in the north, like empty coke crates. Capons, fryers, roasters! all out like hot lights. Not one of them the color of coke.

Cokes today were like chickens. Stiff, silent, cold. One never having lived; the other having one life to give. The memorial was simple. American flags. Texans eating ham, cokes in their hands, surveying chickens, scattered across the land.

Let Me Take You

If I took you over the hills of my life
you would know what I have been looking for
Roamed from Detroit
to Ann Arbor
Hitchhiked up the smelly Pacific down the tail of my feet
for my blood's home
Through the alleys of Albuquerque
irises in gardens
horses grazing in dry pastures
quivering like red apples in fall

If I took you out to what I have known
it would be dying now past recovery
My grandmother
in a nursing home in the middle of New York
The last of us who could tell us who we were
shot through every cell with old age
blind and wanting ice cream
1,000 miles away from the restless storm of her still young skin

Let me take you to the edge of the red ribbon
the violet breeze
let me show you sagebrush rolling in the wind
dead fish floating downstream
let me take you back to the open skull
peach on a mountain
lost river   fallen shoe
aspen leaf quaking in the quiet of the world

Sitting by a Pond in Ohio, Thinking of Japan (1998)

I Tried to Marry America

I tried hard to marry America
To let its rivers swim in me
and the lost small farm graveyards
be the death of my people too

I tried to marry America
the red freckled hand of a man I loved
carried a lit tree into my home in December
I ate scallop stew the body of Christ in the evening

I tried hard to marry the Ohio Valley
and Sandusky County
I tried to bring Cleveland to sit at my table and
eat gefilte fish
to hide the afikomen in Arkansas
and help San Francisco when her kippah fell off
I tried to call in the Shabbas bride over the plains of Nebraska
and break braided egg bread over the Dakotas
To make God of the Universe the majesty of the Adirondacks

I tried to make a wedding band of wheat
and wear the veil of lilacs leaning over a picket white fence
I tried to get the accent off my lips
and wipe the honey from my face

Coming Together

I want to do it in different rooms
I want us to turn out all the lights
even in the heavens
one by one twist those bulbs too
and after traveling up there in the atmosphere
come down to the living room
on a pale blue blanket
Drink beer
till we become shimmering
clicking clear glasses together
and with the pure light of our own
tell stories in the naked heat of summer
We two violets of this worn-out marriage

When I first met you
I thought you were water
sounds traveling down the body
Let's sing such silences
in the motion, I imagine, of elephants
making love under the African sky
or whales rising
out of the center of the Atlantic
coming together on the surface of water
or ants
hundreds of us covering one square of sidewalk
carrying each other over to the grass
Even more joyous
like cokes on a counter in Nebraska
or the stove and refrigerator wanting each other
all day across the kitchen
The ceiling
wings outspread
longing for the floor

I want you in all these ways
then direct as ketchup dropped from the bottle
onto hot steak
or the finger touching ice cubes
Right through our spines and out our teeth
With lungs in full sail
and our chests rising and falling like mountains

Jukebox (1999)

I'd Like To

Drag deep
on cigarettes in lonely cafés
always with cheap coffee
Believe in the straight lines
of plains homes and churches
the dried god on the altar
That my standards were the only ones
besides the whores and rummies

I'd like to be an American
have my teeth turn brown
and run from the parts of my body
below the waist
Own used car lots
that glimmer in the American sun
shop in stores that have strawberries
when snow is on the ground
Enough cattle each person
could eat five cows a year

I'd like to know what it is to be us
See black men sing pure jazz
over the bar stools
Show pigs on their high-heeled dancer hoofs
at state fairs
Letting the real food of the country go stale
behind showcases with blue ribbons
Hold glasses up to the swallowing sea
Worry that our verbs aren't strong enough

And when we die silent to the moon and our dreams
and they put the lid over us
carry us to our native foreign ground

in big cars with big engines
we will remain unknown to ourselves
Our fathers' successes leave us empty
with nowhere ever to go
but on their backs
and into their graves
with the wind
and the songs sailing over us

Small Town Café

When we were married, we'd travel. Go to small town cafés. The white cups thick with coffee and the thin white toast. The bargain breakfasts. I loved the waitresses he loved. Thin ones with thick lips, drenched in some sorrow that reaches back to a lonely Iowa childhood. During breaks she stood at one end of the blue Formica counter, dragged deep on a cigarette, accentuating her cheekbones. She knew how to smoke with the tragedy of America, wore thin white anklets and white canvas sneakers. Eyes like blue bachelor buttons. He thanked them for the fried eggs on the white plate and asked for real milk for his coffee.

I sat opposite him with water in a green transparent glass. I was impatient, dark as a steel nail. You either marry someone just like you or just the opposite. It doesn't matter. You are looking for yourself. I was in love with the glass sugar jar, white napkins in the aluminum holder. I was in love with the painful bare beige wall, the one scotch taped sign curling at the edges, calling for Tombstone Pizza across the narrow room and the call came back to me.

Yes, I loved him. His hands around the fork, the many small wrinkles his lips made when he chewed, the long freckled arm. It was the land I saw all around. The closeness of trees, tired concrete in the sun. The temptation to have a Kit Kat at the glass counter. The slow ride through town, looking for second-hand stores. He bought old pants that looked good in the city. I loved him for who he was.

.

Wall and Window

The airplane moves out of this window into the wall
cutting the ear with its sound
A man in a khaki green hooded jacket
walks bent over down the sidewalk
swinging gold leather gloves
He walks past the sight of this window
into the wall of this room
One small spare sparrow lands
for an instant
A car out of sight starts up its motor
and moves away
The window does not want
to hear what it cannot see
It does not notice the car's motor

Three boys, one in a navy hood,
two with bright cherry hats
walk through the lower half of the window
and continue into the wall
The wall has a heart for sound
and listens to their steps
Some things are silent
Bike wheels way below
A kid's scream if it continues for long enough
Walls are the sight of sound
Two hammering heels below us
walk on wood
Us are you and me
The mind and my hand

All the Midwest

I see your face in a man bending over his steaming coffee
in the corner of a café
I see your legs move down the street
Your hand bow to Buddha in the zendo at 5 a.m.
I walk in your mind's rivers
I talk out of your mouth
I see your foot straighten as you sit in the dull sun
of October, leaning against our house and feeling the wall
and plaster for warmth
I hear you every place there is music
in the sounds of buses   leaves rustling   silver cornstalks

There is no place I can go where
your body doesn't walk in my mind
Down the spine of dry November
through memory of hawk black crow
south of the Mendota Bridge
All the midwest is your mother
the cold the lonely face of yearning
and spring broken through the bounty of wingless trees

House in Summer, Ohio (1998)

Before Your Time

If you don't make friends in May
you'll never make them again

If you don't listen to crickets cry black in the night
you'll never hear them again

If you don't cry in November among lost silver fields
you'll never cry again

If you don't turn the corners of a lake
your car will drive straight forever

If you don't love Butler Drug where the ham sandwiches are thin
you'll ask yourself every day why you live here

If you don't believe there is a poet in the ordinary streets
you'll lament lost elms you'll want to be Jewish
you'll want to buy dark bread

If you don't drive 94 to St. Paul
you'll never remember the taste of raspberries
you'll never love the leaky roofs
the 1,000 green duplexes that line the streets

If you marry before your time
you'll sit lonely in croissant cafés across
from Schlampp's department store
and watch the first October rain fill these streets
with the dark brilliance of coal about to burst into diamonds

Today I sat in front of a judge
and told him about the dissolution of my marriage
under white skies
with the Minnesota River running ice to its December
destination

Yes, Judge, my name was Goldberg before the marriage
and it was Goldberg after the marriage
Mountains are mountains
then mountains disappear in some nameless blue

When the judge asked if I felt everything was fair
I wanted to tell him that I would have liked
the red and white kitchen table
we bought one May for thirty dollars
I would have liked the blue pottery plates
bowls and cups
I would have liked us to keep loving
to find some peace in the morning light of our faces
together

Well, Judge, we met one Shabbas in the elephant house
in hippie New Mexico
Slept under stars where his clarinet ran rivers
up cottonwoods and down old thin streams
Judge, I want you to know we loved
rode across America into unknown towns
tipped the scale of time with old melodies
like starlight and branches slowly bare in October
the rain filled with cedar smoke

Judge, when you told me the petition for divorce was passed
I saw old mesas peyote tepees and the bitter taste of cactus

swim across the courtroom
There is a big life
The Navajos know it
The Jews know it
Buddha knows it

I know where the last minutes of my husband are
They are waiting with me to return
mountains to mountains
and rivers to rivers
and man to woman
one flying low over the City of Angels
and one fair female bird
headed for the cliffs of Galilee   the Red Sea
and the ancient earth beneath

City Moon (1998)

Top of My Lungs

Even though I am unhappy
I come home singing at the top of my lungs
Shovel off the new snow and shove it on the old
Open the useless screened porch door
and take off my big boots
There are fried eggs
yellow as pearls
The old bed I dive into like a warm whale
The phone ringing
that duck on the wall
And even though I am unhappy
I sleep with the peace of flying angels
And even though I am sad
my wallet's empty
I buy the best soap
And even though my heart is hurting
out of sure will
I come home singing with the last night wind
and the first morning star
and the canary
and the summer that was killed below our house

I walk down to the Rainbow Café
call my Catholic friend Mary to come
have a drink and eat a turkey sandwich
The down coat I wear all winter still has the goose feathers
from a hundred flying birds
They let us smoke at our small table
Mary will always meet me here
They fill our glasses with the most sparkling water
for free
and the cold moon rises over the marquee
of the Suburban World theater

So even though I am unhappy
I throw back my old goat throat
and sing slowly
"Oh my darlin' Clementine"
by the beautiful lake in Minnesota
as the pressure of black night cold
moves in on us from all ten directions
I sing to the moon above the lake
"You are lost and gone forever"
calling the pure beast of loneliness down from the sky
with the old American song haunting city lights
"Dreadful sorry Clementine"
and though the very earth has swelled up
like an elephant with pain
I stand on its back singing
in this sad universe
where one lover leaves another for all time
and nothing to say with your feet on the ground

I found him once in the hospital
sitting on the windowsill
looking out on the rain
and the little shabby house in the alley he'd fallen in love with
In his white pajamas and blue striped cotton robe
we walked down the long shiny fluorescent halls
one foot after the other
him holding onto me
He was the smell of iris petals
curling in as they die
the night moon
and the navy blue sky

Before Stars (2000)

Like Nothing Ever Happened

(for Jim Perlman)

I didn't know love couldn't break
  down the walls of everything
Come singing home to daughters
  of the blind blue eyes
I didn't know that it couldn't crumble
  the walls of Auschwitz and Buchenwald
That our fathers couldn't burn down
  the stink in a day
That World War II couldn't come home
  to roost
That our fathers couldn't come out
  the same men
  in love with our red-lipped mothers

I didn't know that the smell of dying japs
  even over a whole century of air
  in bombers above the small island country
  would stink in our fathers' pores
That the army was the only traveling
  they would ever do
  never come home the same men
That the pain in back of their eyes
  was lost in the folds of family

I didn't know that a heart could go out
  and still keep beating
Stare at TV for long hours
  knowing your wife would never believe
  what you saw
  The filth in the eyes of men at war
I didn't know time could stop at World War II
  never grow in tomatoes in future summers

I didn't know our fathers died there
  even if they never lay there
  on the fields with their breathing gone out
That my father 35 years later
  on our porch in the midwest
  could say in dark-eyed stupor of evening
  "I could re-enlist and kill kill kill"

I didn't know
  these men flooded our land
  down the highway of three decades
  with war banging their brains
  silent unseen and tortured
  like grain milled down by stone
I didn't know
  we were the daughters of night guns
That our blood fathers were killers
That the hearts were torn out of us
  in World War II
Came to graze in ice cream parlors
quiet cricket streets
years later
like nothing ever happened

Wanting Men

I fear their size and the tick
of their minds
the measure of death they live with
I believe men are dinosaurs and I want them to live
I want men
I want their bodies above me riding out the horse fields
of night
Their total loss of eyes and sense
when they pour the last of themselves inside me
The way they twitch and sleep
their faces open
at the smell of warm fields
and they want home worse than animals

I like them to pull back their lips
and show their teeth
the color of their ears
The body is their magic rose
I like the way they ride into storms
gallop toward future fields

I fear their earth
and the way they drive
their hands on the steering wheel
and the radio tuned to terrible music

A Girl Sometimes Wonders

A girl sometimes wonders
if her father slept around

I think my father did
I didn't want to believe it
but my father did sleep around

Heaved his body like a cloak
over some female redhead
and poured our seed into her

There were nights
he drank coffee
ate T-bone steak
lots of ketchup
I could taste it
the fat too
wedge of iceberg lettuce
split tomatoes

He left for the bar
rolled a cigar in his mouth
eyed women
their knees breasts
like they never wore a shred of clothing
cash register rang a high pitch
Rheingold neon light turned slowly

He put his paw
over her darkness
she bent her body back in white unfitted sheets
His own daughters watched him pull away
in a Buick through a screen door

They were smut
if they believed he slept around
they taped their mouths shut

Dinner
We ate barbeque out back
spat watermelon seeds across the patio
sucked at summer fruit
at long malt straws

This we knew
no pennies or green seedless grapes
could ever take his place
left a restlessness in us
nothing could replace

Ben Goldberg (1998)

Big Ben

1

Someday I'm going to have to say goodbye to my father
his long jowls
grey face
receding hairline will stop growing
Someday my father will die
    and I hope it's the way he wants—
    holding the winning ticket for a double at Roosevelt
Raceway
    a cigar in his mouth
    his belly full of chichi and pistachio nuts
    bing cherries
    looking handsome and sexy
the rain falling all over Miami Beach
the Jewish cemeteries in Queens well taken care of
His daughters collecting the final payment
for the bar business
from the hack who screwed his wife's friend
and invested
Who changed the old red and green booths by the window
took down the ancient photo of the Bikini Atoll explosion
put up fake wood paneling
over the old flowered walls

My sister and I will roll our blue Buick
up to the red brick Aero Tavern
Tell him our daddy's dead
and we want the money—all of it!
Fill this empty potato chip bag
Right now
with cool $1,000 bills
And we'll chew Wrigley's Spearmint
hard on our back molars
the way my father, Big Ben, always told us not to

and crack it
the way Mrs. Hodges, my friend's mother, did
in her high heels   full skirt   red lipstick
as she stirred the hot soup
after coming home from work

　　　　2
Oh father
we'll all miss you
back in Farmingdale
the bank across from the library
your bar kitty-corner to the drugstore
your slow walk from the parking lot
behind George's Confection at 7 a.m.
Newsday tucked under your arm
thin belt and starched white shirt
Your shame when we came to visit
you didn't want us to see where you worked
the turning lights caught in the whiskey bottles
The sidewalks grey, the winters mild, the summers humid
long row of stores down Main Street
Sam's Army and Navy—the only other Jew
in the town—
his daughter Amy Bernstein married right out of high school

Your two daughters
we didn't know then
how much you loved us
We scattered across the country
like blossoms seeding another land
We didn't know then
that you would grow old
someday die
We thought you would live forever
like the green split level you sold
the one you painted grey
but it was always green

You were a Jew
your father was a Jew
We lit candles for him
and your sweet mother Rose
who died old of Parkinson's disease at 50
Now if we were together
if we weren't feathered across America
We would light candles for Aunt Rae
with her nose job
long legs
and one memory down Oak Neck Lane through the lilacs
For Aunt Lil, the tower woman
in a red mouth and red hair
her rich husband who owned tenements and fraternity houses
for Brooklyn College
For Uncle Sam, your oldest brother—
the one dream of the family that fell

        3
If you wait 14 more years
If you wait till you're eighty
last Goldberg from Russia
last man alive
I'll tell your story in Lincoln, Nebraska
Then Cody, Wyoming
I'll bring you with me!
We'll wear cowboy hats big pointed boots with embroidery
You'll be in the audience when I read about you
you can toss up your hat
stomp your feet
break down and cry through the whole thing
the way you did at my old wedding
and held onto my mother for support
in the backyard of my in-laws' house
in a suburb of Minneapolis
the farthest place you'd ever been in America

among white folks with no Jewish names

You cried again when you and my mother
got back to the hotel
wrapped your arms around each other for the thousandth time
in the white night

We are all going fast through the color of irises
we are all opening into the magic world
we are all moving past willows clouds
past shrubbery and old photos
and nothing can stop us
not even love or our feet
or the absolute will we Jews have
to survive

Sister

Just this last June we were in Milwaukee together, playing
tennis, going to the sand dunes on Lake Superior. We ate at
Benjamin's delicatessen everyday.

But most I remember her in the haunted dark train station, a
paper bag at her feet full of strawberries and melons. She sat
in that thin wood chair with her long hair, face almost like
mine, fuller mouth. There's always one in the family more
beautiful: you give that gift to them and go on.

She sat there sad. She knew I would take the long train up along
the Mississippi into Minnesota. I'd take it alone and we'd
sit in two separate Midwest cities, neither of us having found
our way out of the circle of family in New York, the Sunday
dinners and death of our grandfather. Neither of us would
quite make it through the white clouds of America.

She sat and sighed and at least 500,000 Jewish women in train
stations all over Europe did the same thing not so many years ago.

The Great Tree (1998)

Forgotten Ones

God of Abraham
God of Isaac Jacob
God of Rebecca Sarah Ruth
of Lillian Rosensweig and Aunt Priscilla
with her yellow marigolds in Brooklyn
and the newsstand by the subway entrance
God of Esther planting willows in Long Island
and pink hibiscus in Miami
God of mother Sylvie Ann with her story lid eyes
and the mouth of wonder and her soft miraculous knees
in a cotton nightgown
God of Uncle Manny whitening into old age on his mother's chair

God of the rootless New Yorkers that left New York
God of the rootless Jews who stayed in New York
God of the burning of Poland and the empty Jewish cemetery
in Warsaw
and Elaine's aunt in Queens with the numbers on her left arm
and the *Jerusalem Post* and the candies on the coffee table
God of the lost American Jews who have no god
who stand in the streets of Chicago against a blistering winter
that makes the mouth forget cousin Abraham and cousin Isaac
and the forgotten ones in the army
and the forgotten ones in college
and the forgotten ones in Newark, New Jersey
after the rich moved out to the suburbs

God of lamplight and candlelight
God of roast chicken and freeze-dried coffee
of old rooms in Miami hotels
full of cockroaches and old people in white sheets
God of skylines along the Florida coast
and pale pink and yellow Palm Beach homes

God of murder and suicide
of Gary's grandfather Mr. Stein
whose name in red cursive neon appeared
near my home on Long Island
selling more chrome for your cars
who jumped from his balcony in Pompano Beach at 83
God of his folded body in the hard sand and stopped heart

God of David Solomon Miriam and Rebecca
Mother of earth and small lean yellow salamanders
green covered rocks by the slapping ocean
and swollen feet in the heat of humid summer
God of cars and wheels
of high rises moving out of the earth into the white sky
and the pink sky at dusk
and the grey sky at dawn

And Mother of stars and noon and gull wings
great bands of turkey buzzards in the south
and tennis in the rain
the wet ball like an old dog's yellow face and the puddles
and green trees
And the soft moment we are alive
at the change of the traffic light
and God and Mother of weeping death
tears in eyelashes
Bless Us   Bless Us   Bless Us
through all the rivers of time

New York Body

You know it from my eyes
From my muscles like New York streets
   that have lost their shape
When old buildings collapse in Brooklyn
   and drunks crumble in corners
   my body bends to their sorrow
The white man in front of a Harlem liquor store
   selling the true newspaper of Jesus
   and young lean blacks jive him
He keeps talking not knowing trouble's ahead
My body's blind in this way too
   like a callus
   like the man selling Jesus by rote
My body has the smell of cooked flesh
   the roasted Jewish smell wafted over from Europe
   the dark oils secreting at the beginning of heat
My fingers still have the newspaper smell
   of the *Herald Tribune*
And in the corner pocket of my cotton coat
   you can find a dead plug nickel for the subway

I am the old waiter filling water glasses
   on Delancey Street
The skinny-armed kid on the corner in a striped t-shirt
My body knows the yellow cab and trains taking off
I am women in plaid aprons long ago on summer stoops
   when the tree on the curb shaded a little
   and the garbage can chained to the tree
   didn't smell so bad

Look at my face
   you'll see moles and thin hair
Come closer
   See the pores on my nose
   the chicken pox mark on my right cheek
   a few whiskers on my chin
This is my Jewish face
This is my New York body
   the stooped shoulders and hidden chest
   dodging the violence of men on the streets

Elijah

My friend Elijah never came to my house to drink wine in April
He never bought Oreo cookies or wool socks

Elijah saw birds crack open in the night
and field mice split the sides of mountains

My friend Elijah never got mail, was overweight
or smelled perfume silk or roses

Oh Elijah swayed with shadows
heard the voice where no voice was
saw the fire where it was cool and calm
and shattered in earthquakes where no earthquakes slept

My friend Elijah didn't read the Torah or milk a cow
My friend Elijah bought no salt and never shopped on Saturday

Elijah saw God and came home quiet and still
after evening storms.

She Climbed the Mountain (1999)

When a Jew marries
she marries for all time
She marries her father
and her sons
and Abraham and Israel
She carries their bones
out of the burial places
across the Jordan River

She marries the Judean hills
the rocks the red wild poppies in spring
Her daughters plant seeds for all generations
They put on the veil under the chuppa
and kiss the quiet voice forever

When she comes to bed
her long train of history comes with her
When she touches his face
there are years of wailing in his cheek
and the days of waiting crumble
as his lids close to her kiss

Chair (1999)

Coffee With Milk

It is very deep to have a cup of tea
Also coffee in a white cup
with milk
a hand to go around the cup
and a mouth to open and take it in
It is very deep and very good to have a heart
Do not take the heart for granted
it fills with blood and lets blood out

Good to have this chair to sit in
with these feet on the floor
while I drink this coffee
in a white cup
To have the air around us to be in
To fill our lungs and empty them like weeping
this roof to house us
the sky to house the roof in endless blue
To be in the midwest
with the Atlantic over there
and the Pacific on our other side

It is good this cup of coffee
the milk in it
the cows who gave us this milk
this
simple as a long piece of grass

'48 Plymouth in August (1998)

Boy Who's Cut Every Class Comes to Your Class for the First time

and of his own accord
he goes over to the map
hanging back of your desk
He looks at it
really looks at it
He's following his finger along one path
It's Texas!
He lived down there with his grandparents
by the time they drove halfway through Iowa
he'd be asleep
His granddad would drive through the night
through Missouri Kansas in the summer heat
You'd be glad for store air conditioners

Once we drove to Montgomery, Alabama
you wouldn't believe it was so close
—he follows his finger slowly along the map
like he was traveling—
to visit my dad's people
We come upon a buzzard convention
Big black birds in Louisiana
four or five of 'em
the car drove through 'em
the car covered with buzzards

Blue Piano (1980)

Grape Nuts and milk:
I poured each out of their own container
and ate them together

If we have no soul
something aches
in us anyway

Heaves our breath
pumps our blood

Sun thrown across treetops
Do you see New Mexico?

Windstorms
crack across it
days break
against it

I hurt
for dry dirt
big sky
bell in a tower
sage
across the eye

Burnt land
old sand carcass
your rosebuds
are hardening
your leaves turning
my heart
burning

When I Forget

When I forget an appointment
streets become amnesiac
When I eat apples
it is fall in Venezuela
When I borrow money
the banks in London raise their interest
and when I eat eggs in the morning
all red hens in Kansas call out my name
When my tire is flat Columbus sails off the end of the Earth
and when I cry out in joy
maples in December take back their leaves
and people in bowling alleys roll strikes
and planes turn around
to fly back to LaGuardia

'48 Chevy, Santa Fe (1999)

Remember This Place

If I took you to New Mexico
   your eyes would open for the first time
If I brought you across the Colorado border
    the earth would shatter beneath your feet
    sky would be as deep as a cat's eye
    or the hollow of a skull
You would see pink hills and piñon trees
red chili peppers hanging from vigas in adobe
Smell sagebrush after rain

I'll teach you names of herbs
This is mullein
here with purple flowers is alfalfa
Do not pick rose hips until the first frost
there is yarrow
and there is the yucca plant
Come
I'll give you a little water and
we'll be thankful in this dry land

Take me back to the green chili pizza
dust wind in March
perfect February
back to Arroyo Seco purple mountain
Eloy Maesta's dried apples, ditch behind the orchard
old rusting Fords in the backyard, sheep grazing pigweed
tepee by the stream, my friend Sass eagle eye
the broken fence, our single bed on the flowered rug

If I took you back there
   I would disappear among bread baking in sunlight
   I would smoke out like incense
   I would be a god vanishing

Sprinkle me over the Indian cemetery
   behind the Lujan house
Bring me juniper on May 31st
Leave my car to graze on the Indian land
Go home alone
I will not come back
I will never come back
Take some posole with you
Stop at Josie's on your way out of town
   for the last chile rellenos
Bring back some turquoise

Remember this place
It will visit you
crawl up your spine like a caterpillar
move inside you like breath
Do not look back
Call out to the sky
Circle the earth with your long tail feathers
otherwise the land will never let you go

This Morning

For breakfast
I licked shut
  an envelope

The Last Great Banana Tree (2000)

Letter From New Guinea

(for Steven)

1

How could I get tired of bananas?
    It's like Howard Johnson's—
        37 different varieties

big ones and small ones
    red and yellow
ones the size of your thumb
    to the size of your arm

and wonderful ones to cook twice—
    first, with the skin on
        then rolled on
            fresh ashes

2

All of those animal stories
when I was young
were so abstract

I was so frightened of the forest
when I first came here

But now—
    I am patient with insects
    and things
    and take notice

3

the object of song
is to move men
to tears

the object of crying
is to move women
to song

and when this happens—
 men and women become
 like the spirits of their dead
 like birds

Last Night in Paris (1998)

How Paris Became My City

Sleeping with the Hassid my last night in Paris
he took off his hat when we went to bed
let down his long payas
unpinned his beard that touched his chest
We sat by the Seine in late evening
and when we walked past Notre Dame
he crossed to the other side of the street
I hated the poor windowless room he slept in
in the basement of a warehouse
the French latrine in the courtyard
where I stood in the metal footprints
legs outspread passing my water into the Paris sewers

In the middle of the night closing
the heavy wood door to the toilet
locking it with a skeleton key
I could see the stars up through the five floors
of the center courtyard
I felt my way back into the room the bed
climbed over him
and lifted his sleeping arm over me
The small room filled with the smell of two bodies
a male and a female
in the dark night of the Montparnesse district
We drank terrible Kosher wine out of paper cups
he ate onion crackers
and his tongue and teeth tasted of onion wheat all over my body
and I was very tired

At seven the next morning I left David
we touched each other's faces
He would take the subway to a very old synagogue
to say Kaddish for his mother

The synagogue that had Dachau written in purple spray paint
across the front door
I would walk across the Île de la Cité
to my hotel and American friend from Nebraska
He watched me as I walked toward the river
and one time a block away I turned to look back
he was still watching

I knew as I walked behind Notre Dame
through the pigeons and passed the early policeman—
the only other human being out—
that I would have to let go of everything someday
I was not of any place or time
Right then as I turned the morning corner
onto Rue de Rivoli
I understood how to whistle
You blow through a hole in your mouth
over your lower and out your upper lip
and with the right breath
a little music comes out

Finally any place you live
even in Jerusalem
you want to be offered a glass of hot tea
maybe some round crackers and white cheese
you still want a bath and sleep in the night
you want to fill your body with spring and red anemones

Finally and always we need music
our ears grow thirsty for the wind
and green grass
we want to fill our eyes with human faces
no matter how big the sky is

Even in Jerusalem
we want our lips to form language
500 crawling languages
and we want someone to smile and nod
and accept our foreign coins

Summer 1995 #3 (1995)

Leaving Israel

(for Carol Soutor)

I'm sorry for the empty afternoons when I wanted to go home
   and for the letters I wrote when I could have
   been walking up Zion, down the Kidron Valley
I have had too many cold nights and wind-blown days

I'm sorry Batia and I couldn't have seen each other more
   and I have grown old from being young in these last months
I'll miss the tea in glasses, Tel Aviv far away
   and the lights of too many cities in long distances through
   the night
I'll miss the pale light on the Temple Mount, the mad donkeys,
   bare hills near Jericho and the abandoned dirt Arab homes

Forgive me, Jerusalem, if I did not love you enough, rode your
   buses down the spine of whistling memory, your stones,
   broken cemetery on the Mount of Olives, did not wait centuries with
   you for the pale donkey carrying the Messiah into your
   golden gates
Forgive me for still loving my ex-husband though he is not Jewish
   and the nights I still want him deep in my skin and the
   minutes that have passed blooming irises
The old man begging at the bottom of the underpass at the central
   bus station who I never gave coins to—forgive me, and the
   half light down Strauss after the Turkish baths with the quick
   long-coated Hassids, moving in the dying day like an old song
   down the hill
Forgive me for being modern and still wanting religion and being
   scared alone in the Old City
And forgive my dreams at night that sleep with too many men
   and sit with women for hours in coffee shops in lost streets
   at the edge of town

And forgive me for loving the desert, way beyond sound or thought
sense or my eyes opening, and being too old to move anywhere
anymore

I'm Trying

I'm trying to tell something about empty farm fields
broken by fall
and the half light of sun
cafés in towns with only a gas station, church and bar
I'm trying to say something about loneliness
about the crack of pale yellow cornstalks
in the middle of September in Minnesota

Abstract at Ghost Ranch (1999)

From Taos to Gallup and
Canyon de Chelly

You still come to me like a fresh lover
Woman of brown and pale pink
I should have left everything for you
should have gone so deep into your heart
I'd get lost in yellow aspen leaves
stand on the straw of your autumn

I should never have taken another lover
I should have walked your hills
till my soles burned
till the sky that old dwarf
opened its secrets
till someone stopped whispering your name 1,000 miles away

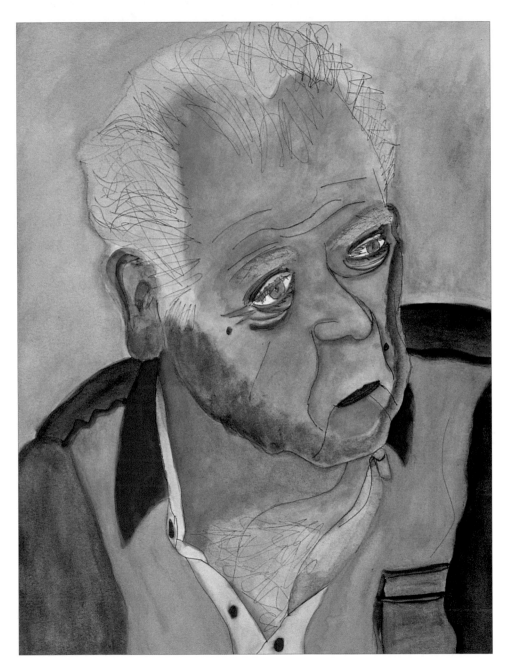

The Victorious Age of 83 (1999)

Where's My Grandfather's False Teeth Now?

Where's my grandfather's
false teeth now?

He kept them
in a cup
in the night

He bites down
on the dirt
in his mouth

One Winter Morning (2000)

Holy Land

I want the earth to last
I want it to last beyond Saturday night
and the onion soup
Out beyond walks in the hills
among wild poppies and black dogs
Past Crusader castles and the Jordan River
past Arab guns and Jewish stubbornness
Through rivers and eucalyptus trees
and white horses standing in tall yellow clover
I want the earth to last

Just Now (1995)

I only know that the Messiah will ride a wild ass
and she'll come down the path
through the Mount of Olives
that oldest Jewish cemetery in the world
and in some high yellow clovered grass outside of Tiberius
next to the Hotel Gat and a small orthodox synagogue
there will be a white horse
who will turn and look at you
and in that moment
the dead will be so tired from their wait
they'll decide not to rise
not today
not this Shabbat
though the steaming soup and browned chicken
in its sacred bones will be waiting on platters
next to the thin Israeli napkins

Still I know when the Messiah comes
she'll want to be here
and not go to Paris
or St. Paul, Minnesota
or Glasgow or Heidelberg
She'll stay in Jerusalem
with her Jews
and everyone at tables in Beersheba and Haifa and New York
will sigh a sad sigh, "We've waited so long"
and we'll eat the dinner of peace
and taste each mouthful slowly
and drink water which will last all night
and the salad and beets and potatoes
will last all night

The violin will play no more mournful songs on the guts of cats
and the Jews will lose their blue souls
and even the number 9 bus will wear daffodils as it shoots
its way up to Mount Scopus
and the clouds will separate
and St. Peter's fish will grow fat and live forever
in the Kinneret, in the Galilee, in the harp lake.

Dream

I was splattered on the floor
in a red silk kimono

The fish store owner
knocked me out!

We argued that he gypped my mom
on a pound of Nova Scotia lox
in Chinatown

This One Great Life (2001)

I Want to Say

Before I'm lost to time and the midwest
I want to say I was here
I loved the half light all winter
I want you to know before I leave
that I liked the towns living along the back of the Mississippi
I loved the large heron filling the sky
the slender white egret at the edge of the shore
I came to love my life here
fell in love with the color grey
the unending turn of seasons

Let me say
I loved Hill City
the bench in front of the tavern
the small hill to the lake
I loved the morning frost on the bell in New Albin
and the money I made as a poet
I was thankful for the white night
the sky of so many wet summers
Before I leave this whole world of my friends
I want to tell you I loved the rain on large store windows
had more croissants here in Minneapolis
than the French do in Lyons
I read the poets of the midwest
their hard crusts of bread dark goat cheese
and was nourished not hungry where they lived
I ate at the edges of state lines and boundaries

Know I loved the cold the tap of bare branches against windows
know there will not be your peonies in spring
wherever I go
the electric petunias
and your orange zinnias

The Oak and the Owl (2000)

Into This World

Let us die gracefully into this world
like a leaf pressed in stone
let us go quietly breathing our last breath
let the sun continue to revolve in its great golden dance
let us leave it be as it is
and not hold on
not even to the moon
tipped as it will be tonight
and beckoning wildly in the sea

Self-Portrait (2000)

About the Author

NATALIE GOLDBERG is the author of many books, including *Writing Down the Bones, Wild Mind, Thunder and Lightning*, a memoir, *Long Quiet Highway*, and a novel, *Banana Rose*. More of her paintings can be viewed in her books *Living Color: A Writer Paints Her World* and *The Essential Writer's Notebook*.

Natalie lives in northern New Mexico. She teaches retreats on writing and Zen practice. For more information on her workshops and painting exhibits, please visit her website at www.nataliegoldberg.com.